Word Pictures Etched in My Head

poems

James Lawson Moore

Copyright © 2019 James Lawson Moore

Cover Design: Stephen H. King ("TOSK")
Stock Image and Initial Cover from Canva.com

Author Photo: Eric Cline

This is a work of fiction. Names, characters, businesses, places, events, locales, and incidents are either the products of the author's imagination or used in a fictitious manner. Any resemblance to actual persons, living or dead, or actual events is purely coincidental.

No part of this book may be used nor reproduced in any manner whatsoever without written permission, except in the case of brief quotations embodied in articles and reviews. For more information, email all inquiries to...

jamemo2@mail.regent.edu

All rights reserved.
ISBN: 978-1-7343578-0-6

FIRST EDITION

A MEANDERING DEDICATION

I wrote the majority of the poems in this book during a bout of intense creative energy; I ended up completing much of the first draft in a week and some days. I did this while sitting on top of a previous book I had just completed (I needed to distance myself from that first book so that I could go back to it with fresh eyes). That first book is decidedly angrier, more confused, emotionally charged and in general a meandering tome that goes all over the place. Which oddly enough those things came together in such a way as I ended up enjoying the work when I went back and read over it. But that doesn't change the anger and the wandering out in the wilderness that exists within the pages of that first book (which will, by the way, end up being published after this one). I needed a chance to step away from it and move on in another place creatively. My heart, mind and soul needed that chance.

    Yes, I was depressed. I was so far gone with the way my life was going that I was having suicidal thoughts again. I don't enjoy saying these words, but they are the truth and I speak them that others may know that they are not alone in their mental hell. We are doomed to the flames together. I stand with you, and I will fight with you until the day when we can storm the Pearly Gates together. And I pray that you find your inner peace just as I have found here, in my art and in my work.

Over the course of several days, specifically those first few days when I started writing these poems, I had the chance to reexamine my life. And I came to the conclusion that my problems don't define me. I am completely and utterly myself, even with the flaws that would be better suited in a character of an Elizabethan tragedy. If I were to have a message for those who suffer just like me, it would be this: you are not the sum total of your faulty parts. Rather you are a prince among men, an angel among weeping willows—a person with the stardust leftover from the Creation of the Universe running through your veins. You matter, even though the one looking back at you in the mirror is trying to tell you something different.

So I guess what I'm saying is that if you are like me, and the ghosts are hammering at your skull to tell you that the pain is all there is, then this book is dedicated to you. Here's a toast to you, and here's rooting for you kid. I love you.

James Lawson Moore

My father never missed a drink in his life. Or a joint. Or a party. Or a chance to get laid. He also never missed a day of work, or a house payment, or a car payment. I never went hungry, although he did a couple of times so I wouldn't. This is a man who survived four heart attacks. The doctors revoked his organ donor card and issued him a "Hazardous Waste" decal.

—Christopher Titus

"*The world is like a ride in an amusement park, and when you choose to go on it you think it's real because that's how powerful our minds are. The ride goes up and down, around and around, it has thrills and chills, and it's very brightly colored, and it's very loud, and it's fun for a while. Many people have been on the ride a long time, and they begin to wonder, "Hey, is this real, or is this just a ride?" And other people have remembered, and they come back to us and say, "Hey, don't worry; don't be afraid, ever, because this is just a ride." And we ... kill those people. "Shut him up! I've got a lot invested in this ride, shut him up! Look at my furrows of worry, look at my big bank account, and my family. This has to be real." It's just a ride. But we always kill the good guys who try and tell us that, you ever notice that? And let the demons run amok ... But it doesn't matter, because it's just a ride. And we can change it any time we want. It's only a choice. No effort, no work, no job, no savings of money. Just a simple choice, right now, between fear and love. The eyes of fear want you to put bigger locks on your doors, buy guns, close yourself off. The eyes of love instead see all of us as one. Here's what we can do to change the world, right now, to a better ride. Take all that money we spend on weapons and defenses each year and instead spend it feeding and clothing and educating the poor of the world, which it would pay for many times over, not one human being excluded, and we could explore space, together, both inner and outer, forever, in peace."*

— Bill Hicks

You know, I'm sick of following my dreams, man. I'm just going to ask where they're going and hook up with 'em later.

— Mitch Hedberg

That's my only goal. Surround myself with funny people, and make sure everyone has a good time and works hard.

— Joe Rogan

ACKNOWLEDGMENTS

My parents, Woody and Janice Moore, provided me with the time, encouragement, and space to write in between bouts with the dogs and weekend dinners. They don't always understand what I do, but they seem to respect it as much as any non-writer understands (I mean that as a high compliment).

Eric Cline, my best friend from my community college days, palled around with me in the bookstores and late night dives of Midlothian and Richmond and discussed life with me. An artist in his own right, he took the author photo that appears on the back cover of this book. I owe him more than I will ever be able to repay in this and the next life—you can check the receipt if you don't believe me.

Stephen H. King, a brilliant writer of fantasy who goes by the moniker "The Other Stephen King," answered the call when I was struggling to finalize the cover due to technical issues (I couldn't get the size of the dang file right no matter how many times I adjusted it). He refused to take money for it, asking only for a paperback copy for his troubles. How can I say no to a sweet deal like that?

The great poet and novelist Leah S. Jones turned me on to the website Canva.com, on which I started playing around with the initial cover design. I ended up butchering the final product and needed to bring Stephen in to assist in the fourth quarter, but I still garnered some excellent stuff from which Stephen was able to create something brilliant. She deserves as much respect as anybody, as a writer and as a friend.

Besides these cats I have largely you as the reader to thank for taking part in and digging my work. Without you as a participant I'd be screaming into an echo chamber over here. No artist likes screaming into an echo chamber — they have to have a set of ears besides their own in order to have anything worth doing. So I thank you, and I have to check the receipts over and over again just to prove to myself that this isn't a dream. It is reality, and I am living a good life in the here and now.

1

Start with your people;
ask each and every one
of them what turns them on,
in that one specific hour when

the night meets with day,
and love was just this
whole other thing

that we talk about when we
don't want to fill ourselves
with the silence that feeds off
of those awkward parts
of human interaction.

(9/6/19)

2

Help yourself to love and friendship,
and offer me something in return —
everything, anything, something to make me
smile like a second draft of the Mona Lisa...

(9/6/19)

3

You don't have to say you love me,

but that don't mean that you are entitled

to lie to my face when I come

around asking you for answers to things we never discussed,

that needed answers and were instead left devastated by

the blatant neglect and the secrets

lurking in the deep

and underground.

You don't owe me anything,

but then why go out of your way

to pretend like we aren't joined at the hip

after so many nights spent shouting at the moon

and then asking for the morning to grace

us with some kind of sign

that tells us to go ahead

and confess our sins before

turning in to the deep
and underground.

(9/6/19)

4

You are like Goldilocks with a southern edge,
looking for a love that tastes just right
and coming up empty just before the family
that you did not want to see comes back
into your life and tells you that

every little thing in your life is about to
change (for better or worse—nobody knows—
but it beats going down the yellow-brick road

and running into the Big Bad Wolf
right after he got done with the Three Little Pigs
and the Three Billy Goats Gruff, on his way
to make a date with grandmother; surely

to ruin Red Riding Hood's weekend plans).

(9/6/19)

5

I'm not asking
for much.

All I want to know is that
the love I have to
give to you was worth the journey
it took to get to your apartment

from three states away —

I want to be on the
same page as you,
where we read

alternating sentences that lead us
to many of the same conclusions.

If I could kiss you under-
neath the weight of the
hot summer weather; I want to bed
down next to you in the patch

of swamp grass we found

leading into here,

and I want to trace the
curves of your spine
until we both fall asleep.

And before I forget, I always wanted
just to live out my most vivid dream
with you — you know, the one where we
learned to dance by testing out every

awkward footfall until
we made it absolutely perfect.

Is that really so much to ask for?

(9/7/19)

6

That other boy trying to flirt
with you is a clown—
you were born of royalty, fighting with
monsters and men and things which
dance clumsily up and down

the kingdom—but I recognize you
for what you value above all else, and
I would dare to play the jester
just to endear you to me evermore.

(9/7/19)

7

Heartache is a preexisting condition,
and the only thing that can
cure it is to take you out to dinner and
maybe a few playful winks between
the previews at the Friday night
late show at the Metroplex —

yes, I will admit to coming on
just a little too strong; we've been
going at it for hours, talking over every
detail of the greatest love story as it

plays over and over again in
my head (like the image of you coming
over to my place for a little nightcap
and perhaps a few kisses before
we find an alternative to

falling asleep the next few hours).

Yes, heartache is a terrible disease,

but there are ways of addressing it
and I am trained on every one—

just call me the Doctor of Love,
for I have been readying to
operate to the best of my ability
just to provide you with comprehensive

care, and even an affirming word or two
that can entice you to sign on with me.

So how about it—may I try and heal you now?

(9/7/19)

8

I've been up all night
sending messages to ghosts;

words uttered discreetly to friends who've
moved on to other things and other
homes across state lines, but I still miss them
and the things we said when the silent
spaces got to be too much and

we needed something to make it
just a little better for us (and yes, I might
just be a little melodramatic, but so what?).

Now everyone is scattered across the four winds
leaving me struggling to remember when I ever had
it so good as I did that night when we spent
countless hours dissecting old movies

and drinking coffee that was a tad strong.

I long to go to that place again,

but whenever I go to those
old haunts they seem alien to me —

the coffeeshop where all the cool cats
worked on their latest poems,
are now virtual ghost towns where even the workers
have changed over and the fresh faces don't know
what exactly it is that I'm looking for.

But I still yearn for a human connection;
the bigger the connection, the better.

So now I sit alone, composing love letters to
each and every one of them, just
waiting for the day when we can all get back
together again, and celebrate our lives like

we used to do, when everything was yet green.

(9/7/19)

9

Are you awake?

Jim Morrison and Jesus the messenger
would both like to know before they set up
for the big tent revival on the far end
of town — Jesus has a sermon

he's been dying to try out, while Jim's
just happy to be out working again.

Are you awake?

Every word of every dream you ever had
has been etched into your brain,
and plays on repeat from now until the far end
of eternity — words of love over hate and the
goodwill of man even in the worst of times

when it even becomes difficult to
stand up in the morning, or to
even look at the one in the mirror

for fear of what he might say about you.

Are you awake?

Jim Morrison and Jesus the messenger
would like to have a word with you
about some of the things you have been saying
to your friends and family regarding the state

of the world (what with
the lack of love and trust).

This isn't about some kind of messianic
complex — or even trying to become champion
of the world — rather it's about simply being

at peace with the one in the mirror,
who won't stop telling jokes in order to
keep the beast at a distance and
the hunger safely out of mind
for five more minutes.

Ah, but it almost morning, almost too close

to morning, and the world waits for no one—

are you awake?

Will you wake up
now that we've something
to actually talk about?

(9/8/19)

10

You don't have to
be here all day
for them to know you
care about them
more than

pretending that the
distance between you
only minimally
affects you
and the time spent
keeping apart no

longer hurts you like hell—
it's always best to start fresh.

(9/8/19)

11

You can still be
introspective
on stage, without having
to reveal any of that
or to even hint

at it with vague commentary,
jokes without beginnings or
please for just 5 bucks for drinks.

No one has to know
that you get to a
safe place where you can smile
requires a few near-death scares

and a couple nights spent crying.

And that's ok,
because everything comes
together near the end
of the performance,

when everyone sees
that you were

being real with them
and can forgive all else.

(9/8/19)

12

I told her that I wanted
to swap mom jokes
with Freud before I left for
dinner; she smiled at this

and guided me down well-worn
paths, to her favorite shelf where
her old friends were housed

in between paperback sheets and
embraced in dreams spilled
in black on white (she liked to take
long drinks of $100 words while
she worked, getting trashed

on fresh ideas displayed
at just the right time).

(9/8/19)

13

You like to make snide comments
about God and Dave,
seeming to forget that God took him from
herding sheep in the south fields, and
made him a king as well the lineage
by which came the child Jesus…

(9/8/19)

14

The fachan is a Scottish monster
with one eye, one hand, one leg
and one foot, prowling the country side until
he snatches up and eats the unicorn for lunch—

whether he did it to satisfy his hunger
or out of genuine hate is anybody's guess.

I read where somebody wrote
down a conversation between
some kid and his grandfather, talking about
the lack of a second hand: "That's just
horrible," said the child;

"There are worse things," said the grandfather.

"You could be missing a heart child,"
he added, groaning, "then were
would you be?"

And I guess that would be the worst

thing; whether you are hungry or
just need a change in attitude.

(Inspired by the comic book Bus 900, *written by Christine Sloan Stoddard and illustrated by Laura Bramble.)*

(9/8/19)

15

You want to play with the form and
scream at the top of your lungs just for
the pure hell of it.

The animal must be subdued
before you rise up and
strike the page with a vodka mix of
love and unabated raw hunger
grasping at your innards

like some stranger's lingering kiss.

You want to dance with the words
before they start demanding that you
make love to them, one by one.

The peace of mind you thought you'd get
from scratching out the eye
doesn't come for 3 weeks, and even then
you don't get half of what you expect

so you might as well

do what makes sense to you

under the flickering glow of candlelight.

You want to take care of yourself,
but at the same time you must
dance like hell

even when they pull out all the sheet
music and attempt to force
you to go at it silently — but you
go at it bravely with grace
like a river, because

to do otherwise would be an
insult to the band.

(9/8/19)

16

God created the world in
7 days…well, more
like 6 days followed by a day
of rest to enjoy his work.

I work a single day
and need probably 3 or 4 days
just to get over it — there's
not much I enjoy anymore

but I do like the fact that
for everything there comes
a season, and even though it may
not feel like it good things are coming.

(9/8/19)

17

I draw the ice-covered glass
to my lips and drink
down to the last measure; I start
feeling giddy late in the night,

but I'm happy because
she told me she would
marry me…

(9/9/19)

18

It's a strange world to live in,
but I continue with it
due to the fact that the alternative isn't
really that appealing and I have this

tradition of finding new
ways to live another couple
of centuries (and then
maybe allow a couple

of robots to take up the slack
from there, reworking the
ways of the world
until we're all free).

(9/9/19)

19

Encounter space,
explore those unchartered lands —
but don't come home late.

(9/9/19)

20

If you don't feel it,
did it really happen?

She never stayed over, never
left an article of clothing
or even bothered to try and placate
your inner voice when it tells you
that she was never here to

begin with;

every one of your friends
has told you to tread lightly and
never let down your guard, but
whenever they speak

you'd just know it was time
to completely ignore them.

But I'm not like your other friends,
and I won't waste your time

with little white lies —

she isn't yours

and she was probably
never yours to begin with;
she was fun for a time
but the moment

has passed and now's the time for
each to go their separate ways
before it gets too late

and the both of you go crazy.

If you don't feel it,
did it really happen?

Does it matter?

(9/9/19)

21

You told me to
forget about
kissing you under the steps
of the library,
but that's the one thing
I want to remember
from here to the
bookend of
eternity.

(9/10/19)

22

Dementia-rattled dreams,
followed by days of wondering
through 40-years sands
as though searching for some
Promised Lands…

We all remembered the time when
she still had juice left in the tank;
now everybody's running on fumes and
doctors keep filling our heads with
empty promises telling us
it will all get better.

I don't want to
remember her like
this —

not while the dreams
take over
and the days are as
noncompliant as the

shifting of sands.

She had much more to offer
than some watered-down road map
leading us to some old façade
passing itself off as the
genuine Promised Land.

Were there such a thing
it would fill her tank back
up with what had been taken from her
and we could all be happy pilgrims

on our way to the mountain.

(9/10/19)

23

Kurt Vonnegut liked to say
that we are what we
pretend to be, so we had better
be careful what we pretend
to be.

As a philosophy
it doesn't count
for much,
but there's a lot of
truth to it that
must be

considered—

people like to talk about
what people are doing,
but not so much about *why*
they do it,

and it would seem to me

that the logic behind

what went down the first time would

go a long way in lessening the

damage on the next

go-around.

(9/10/19)

24

We don't give anything
away for free —
everything comes for the right
price, even the art and soul
that went into the thing

you wanted from me to
begin with, that first got you
interested in my view on life.

Every dollar I get goes back into
the life spent living out those experiences
informing the work I do;
all the lies and half-truths that

seek to butcher me from the inside
out, but now they're a part of the story.

We don't just do things
because we think
they're cute — we do them

only because we know of
nothing else of

value by which to
make our living
or even to buy our smokes.

Because this is the deal we've made—

at least, this is the deal
that I have made
when I decided to go out and
give it everything I have

before the next chapter in my life
dictates my next money-grab gig.

(9/10/19)

25

Every room you're in,
you're competing
with the ones who had come there
before — you're not hoping
to be loved

so much as you just want to
be taken seriously as an artist, a performer
who struggles to keep on the same as them

and even as a fellow human
coming here today,
looked the others in the eye and said,
"I am here and I've something finally

to say to you."

That's why you are doing
by coming up on this stage.

(9/10/19)

26

You can try taking the southbound train
through the heart of Georgia,
but no matter how far you go there can only be
so many miles between you and her and the

love you shared so briefly
it was thought to have been lost
forever.

After a while you will learn to find peace
within yourself as opposed to through some other
heart for which you have
no control and which can
only cause more heartache

when she discovers that your souls are
just too far apart to make the intimacy work.

The fine line between
pleasure and pain is close to
splitting at the smallest

little impulse; it would be wise

not to tempt fate and
go on to something else,
something more
rewarding and

perhaps even a little healthier
for you.

Distance can be a difficult thing,
but when your love is
met with emotional absence even a few states
apart won't ease the pain, so you might
just as well work on yourself and

see if you could find those
things you thought were
lost in transit.

(9/10/19)

27

I am starved for affection,
and only by your hand
will my hunger be sated before
the end of the night, when
all bets are off.

(9/10/19)

28

*(18 years ago,
and it still gets to me…)*

I am supposed to be both sad and angry today.

I'm supposed to wake up screaming
at the voices screaming back
from the inside of my skull, at least until the
smoke clears and the deaths are counted.

Nobody's able to talk today
without remembering
back to the day

when the hands of the doomsday
clock were moved to midnight—

everyone's still a little scared of flying,
and too much security
means none at all because the ones
put in charge have no idea

what they are doing

and the deaths are still being counted.

And I'm supposed to
be both sad and angry today,
unable to speak because I'm

screaming at the voices
that are screaming back at me.

I don't know who to trust, and ignorance
seeks to destroy us before the planes
beat them to it and sink us into
our graves, down in the rubble.

But what can I do, and who do I talk to?

I can no longer afford
to be sad or angry;
all can I do is try and survive

despite what was initially done to us
and how it made us dislike each other

in the aftermath—

death rode on a horse to doom us all,
with hell following close behind and
each of us must decide to look

him in the face and say, "You won't do me in today."

(9/11/19)

29

Would you change your mind about me

if I gifted you the moon today,

or would you ask for the receipt to return it and

then tell me about this other guy and the sun?

(9/11/19)

30

What's worse than
unrequited love?

Going about your days, months and
years marching towards the end
of your life while choosing to ignore the signs
that your best friend, who has been by your side

for a few dozen years and who
always wants to be around you
might actually be the right one?

That might actually be the worst thing of all.

(9/11/19)

31

Looking to reconnect
with brothers from your past,
never knowing that
the family has all but died

and the reunion has turned
into a memorial service.

You have to keep a delicate balance
between revering tradition and
refusing to go backwards

in time —

nobody is telling you to disrespect
the memory of those who've
come before, but we have got to come out
of this mindset that all good things have

already happened and
strive for a brighter tomorrow.

Because tomorrow is going to be a better day.

(9/11/19)

32

What are you willing
to accept when the
ax comes to drop and the
night shifts into day with-

out anyone really working
to see what happened
between the intervening hours
when so much was up in the air?

(9/11/19)

33

I never wanted
to hate myself—
every moment I spent
deluding myself was
another moment
spent away

from freedom,
but this prison
won't keep me in
so long as I
keep moving forward
and keep inspecting
these bars for

weaknesses in
the metal.

(9/11/19)

34

I could have told her
how much I loved her
at any time before
the end of her life.

Something always stopped me
from saying those words out loud,
but I always figured I could
wait until a later date.

It was a matter of
good intentions,
and now here I stand on the
road to hell, wishing I had

switched places with her before
everything came crashing down
and she went from daily naps
to the eternal sleep.

Words have no real weight,

no true physical form or
even a real voice of their own —
but they have so much power over

us, and their absence can
wreak havoc on the simplest of
situations (if only hindsight
could help to clean up the mess).

I should have told her those words
before she left from there;
the fact that she more than likely knew
does little to help, and I'm gasping for air.

I never said those words,
preferring that my actions speak
for themselves; if she knew
she will surely tell me once I

greet her on the other side,
where words take on greater meaning
and love is shown rather than spoken —
God, but I hope she'll understand.

I hope she'll understand.

(9/11/19)

35

No more distractions.

This time you must take up your burden
and get out there to complete
what was already started at the beginning of
your life, when everything was still green.

You have got to free your mind
from the prison it has built for
itself — break the lock

and take yourself out into the sunshine.

Everything boils down to how much you are
willing to do in order to
sharpen the blade and maintain that healthy
place between caring and not caring,
where all you have to do is

finally get the work done —
just get it done and

then you will
know peace.

No more distractions—

you have to get down
on it and just do it, do it right
and do it now so that when

it's done no one can
take it away from you.

(9/12/19)

36

Maybe he's in trouble
and that's why he prays.

Perhaps he felt like he never
caught a break in
life, and he figured that maybe a
few nights with the priest at
the downtown church

would do him some good.

Or do you think that he was
worried that God sold him over to
the man who runs the fiery lake,

and he wants to make nice
in order to get out of it?

Whatever reason it is, I can't help
but question the motives
of a man who is not me, who once told me

to go jump in a bucket for all he cared,

who now claims to have a change of heart.

And maybe I'm just
a little bit bitter, because I
knew him for so long and

still feel a certain type of way
about how everything went down between
us as far back as three years ago, when
we were fighting over a girl

who ended up going

with another guy and moved away
(isn't that how it always works?).

Maybe I'm the one in trouble
and in need of praying
to whatever God that would listen to
what I have to say, regarding the
heart and the mind and

the moth and the flame.

(9/12/19)

37

You wanted to fight in Pharaoh's army

immediately after God hit him

with that final plague concerning all those firstborn kids,

and you wonder why I question your survival skills.

(9/12/19)

38

Twenty miles from home, with
endless drumbeats rattling
around in my head

from the party I just left—
she met me there, and now she's
with me and asleep in the

passenger seat (I think she got
too far into the scene, song notes
entering her brain and

making my job of seducing her
away from the guy she was with
all the easier).

We are all just passengers here,
trying to find the right moment to
break away from yesterday

and seek shelter in the autumn fields

of tomorrow — I am moving slower

than the rest of them, and that's ok.

So long as the drum beats

ease off somewhere along mile 21

and the music changes to some-

thing a little more fitting to the

moment I want to create for her,

it will all be ok.

(9/12/19)

39

It was a tradition of the family to
shout over one another
during the holiday meals, and then turn
around and share in laughter and
love while singing old carols
to the holiday wreath
on the door.

Might seem like nonsense to
some of you who haven't heard
of some things,

but even in dysfunction we are functioning,
and even with all the shouting we know
there's a healthy dose of love
somewhere in there.

Still it would be nice sometimes
if we could tone down the hysterics for
just long enough to hear each other
out — the words get lost in

translation, and the food

grows cold by the time we're done.

(9/12/19)

40

Yes I still fight the wiring,
the whisper in my ear trying to speak
comforting lies to me, telling me

that not only should I not go
quietly into that good-
night, but that I shouldn't be going at
all until I get my affairs in order
(whatever that means).

Those lies were a godsend…at first.

Now I put on my headphones and
drown out the noise — I take stock of every-

thing, down to the last detail,
and I learn how to fight against the
mechanism that I can make
for myself the grandest symphony

to play for me a loving song.

Somewhere I've heard that melody before...

(9/12/19)

41

I don't do modern art for the sake
of doing it—
my father and his friends like to call me out
for being an ironic hipster with no sense
of history, background or knowledge

of the things I am fighting
against in the ripped-out
pages of my old
coloring books.

What does he know? He only watches cop shows.

He likes to read cozy mysteries
after long days spent
explaining the scriptures to his flock;

an intelligent man, he still likes to take
out his mind and place it on a shelf
every now and again
just like the rest of us,

only sometimes he doesn't bother
putting it back in its rightful place.

Sometimes I do the same thing when
listening to comedy albums
or sculpting imaginary beings out
of the Mecklenburg red clay
(there's so much of it

from the last time we went down
to grandma's for a reunion).

I am so much like my old man
that even my differences don't seem
so much like differences

and I'm thinking that maybe he would've liked

to have been an artist if life
didn't take him down
a different path —

you know the one, that road

paved with good intentions.

(9/13/19)

42

Can't sleep, don't fit in,
tries too hard and receives so little.

Words get thrown about; love becomes a currency to
be spent on cheap nights and the
nights become addictive to a point where the day starts to look
like the worst buzzkill in the history of the world and mankind.

Depressive sinkholes become
all too common, and you can
fall and remain there

if you aren't mindful of your surroundings.

The ravages of time can cause deep
pains on the uninitiated;
anything can happen now — it usually
does — and nobody would be able to
help because they would've

gotten it too and it can take so much from the body that   the
body won't know that it has only a few seconds of
oxygen left before burnout.

But I don't mean to scare anyone off.

The impulse is strong, but if you are prepared
you can managed to fight
against it; the night and the lack of sleep can
only take from you the things that

you choose to give,
so guard yourself

but don't become blind to the good that
remains as you seek to understand
all that comes and all that

breaks and falls away.

Because it does get better—it did for me, and it will for   you.

(9/13/19)

43

You don't want to be seen as some kind
of punk rock wannabe, or even
the worst kind of ironic hipster cliché who wants
all of the figurative glory without any of the
work that actually goes into it…what

you really want is to do the things
that you believe in, the things that
inspire you to wake up in the

morning and get out into the world where people
refuse to be anything other than
genuine (authenticity is the key, the key to everything
including art, and life, and performing, and taking it

to where it wants to go
no matter the destination.

(9/13/19)

44

Pick up the phone and
call the ones you haven't heard from
in more than two or three months —

you really should've been
keeping tabs on them all along,

but time always provides you with enough
excuses, and now we have reached
a critical moment where your friends are scared,
suffering and seeking to end their loneliness

at the end of a gun.

Go and check on them before
it gets to that point,
before they lose hope and close the circuit
on the loneliness, and the silence, and
everything that goes in between

the two of them — so

call them, call them

no, help to

bridge the gap between the

night and the storm.

(9/13/19)

45

The library isn't as quiet
as it used to be,
isn't pure and self-contained like it's
supposed to be at 3 in the afternoon

(when the place
is populated by the grand-
dads who talk too loud

and bubbly little soccer moms toting around
their crying kids on their way to pick
up the latest self-help book that's supposed to rework
every rough spot in their perfect marriage that
proves to be not so perfect after all).

It took me three years
just to get the one

good study room (with the lighting that
doesn't fail every couple of seconds)
and I'll be damned if

I let them keep me from getting anything done.

My library was my sanctuary —
she was my sunken kingdom and I was
her deposed dictator
seeking just to stay on a couple more hours

until it was time to close.

I start listening to jazz music playlists and just
try to ignore the chaos that exists
right outside my door — I write sonnets to the chaos
and set them to the theme music from those
cheap movies I checked out before

settling in for the day (my art
became my saving grace).

Outside it's still a sojourn into mayhem;
granddads learning how to get with the times and
mothers trying to make time
slow down for just long enough to catch their breath.

I don't pay any of them the attention
they desire; the dethroned king has work
to do, and he's going to do it.

The king is going to do it.

(9/13/19)

46

Give me the
truth;
maybe tell
me things that
only you
would know
so

that I can have
something to
share with
you.

(9/13/19)

47

Sometimes you have to
play the hand you're dealt,
but that don't mean
that you can't try and cheat

when the guy at the
end of the table
isn't looking—he's been
cheating for decades

and would probably
reward you for showing
initiative and for
simply trying.

(9/13/19)

48

I read somewhere that
ole Hank Bukowski
liked to refer to himself as
nothing more than a
wounded lion,

and it took me a while
to really get what
he was saying.

Hank was a
misanthropic writer who
liked to talk a lot
of trash; every word he

ejaculated onto the
secondhand sheets
he got from the dollar store
spelled out so much
trouble for his
professional and romantic

life, but he never

cared so long as
he could publish on the
walls of downtown LA.

Who would've thought that
the man who liked to
yell and scream so much could
find all those tender moments
in between the passages
where he raged

against the women
who smartened up
and left?

Somewhere along the way
he must've sensed that
he needed to clean up his act
and get back to work;
the problem was that
his demons liked

to push him closer
to the edge,
and no man lasts for long
when the voices sing
softly in his ear.

Lions who get
wounded out in the wild
have a hard time
assimilating back
into their prides;

men and women have
much of the same problems —
some more than others,
and a few most of all.

Ole Hank liked to
refer to himself as a
wounded lion;
I guess that's why he liked
to rage against the page.

(9/14/19)

49

28 year old white male, a writer,
maybe a little unsure of himself and
trying to find the words to
justify his existence.

Poetry swirls around in his head
like sperm cells trying to
reach the egg in time to leave a mark;
he goes to write some of it down
and ends up butchering the

job because he's not fully awake and
he needs something to settle his
shaking hands.

28 year old white male, a writer,
composing love notes before he leaves
for work down at the back
room of the Chesterfield public library;
nobody has taken him up on his
offer for endless nights of

serious romance — but
he's gotten used to
the solitude and

it helps with
the writing, so he
don't mind much.

What it all boils down to is this:
the respect for the word
goes above all else — the reverence for the word
takes on an almost religious significance and

nothing else matters
other than the word
when the word is good.

(9/14/19)

50

I don't know that I believe in
alien abductions—
we have enough trouble keeping up with
everything that goes on within our
ozone layer, so we have no

reason to venture out into
the stars and seek the faces of
beings quite different
from those of us down here.

Honestly,
I would rather venture
out into things that are
more grounded and
well known.

(9/14/19)

51

Just as I am,
where every strength and
fault I will reveal
right away, before I even
get up to greet you —

funny how the
only things that keep
coming back to me are
the bad stuff.

My neck scar, from the night
when I attempted to
hang myself, but I had the
sudden impulse not to
actually go through
with it (which
seemed to
scare me more).

These marks on my wrist

are from when I would
cut myself

(I learned that
my blood type was O positive—
the universal donor).

For every one of
these negatives you could
find a positive
to the story, some moral or
happy ending to the
story that is me;

I'm no angel, but I learned to
navigate through the mines
that threaten to take

everything in the back
room of my mind.

I never thought I would
survive the mess I made,
but here I am to

write everything down
and even annotate it

for you

(I got good at
taking notes
and at making notes
on the original notes).

Guys like me who make
the turn-around
eventually bring it
back to God —

for me it was a matter of making my peace

every morning I wake up, still
alive and even glad for it.

This is me, just as I am;
my past is not good
and my future's still uncertain, so
I have to take it day by day.

That's all there is, just the day by day.

(9/14/19)

52

There are only so many words to use
when trying to let go of someone who
might've seemed cool at the start
but who now struggles to carry
her baggage down the street.

I had my share of baggage
at the start of our relationship,
so it's not like I'm accusing her

of things I haven't done many times before —

probably more than anything I want
just to grand her some peace
even as I start walking away and seeing to
my own affairs (affairs I've been neglecting

due to the needs of one
I cared for but couldn't save).

There are only so many words to say goodbye:

only so many ways to tell her that
love isn't enough of a reason
to continue with this thing we created
and then promptly lost control of
when the fights got too big

and the hole we dug
got too deep.

There are only so many words to say
'I love you but we can't
keep doing this' — when the baggage gets
to be too heavy and the love starts

losing its edge you've got to
cut ties and let her go with
the least amount of

damage possible.

Because you were able to talk yourself
into this; now's the time to do the right thing.

But it's so hard, and I

have so much hate within me;

am I strong enough to go through with it?

(9/14/19)

53

A man could be crying
for three days straight, but then on
the fourth day he wonders where

he forgot his car keys and
everything starts over for him.

(9/14/19)

54

In order to
free yourself
you have to be
uncomfortable
and still find
something
out of it

that works to your
benefit later on
down the road

(this isn't
just a first draft
of a Hallmark
greeting card —

I'm being
serious with you
right now, telling
you things that

I wish some-
body would've
told me).

You have to
take risks
while still holding
on to that thing
that made you
want to put your-
self out there
to begin with;

be open but
cautious,
loving but
wise,

working
towards that
golden glow of the
showroom light,
beckoning
you to the front

of the show

and telling you
that to do it
would change your
life forever.

Who knew it would
be so good?

(9/14/19)

55

I never counted on
being a jazz singer;
all I needed was a good hook
to convince her to come back

to me and I'll be
good because I'd
have all I need and
nobody could take it

from me (*the way she dances*
to subtle drumbeats hitting
close to her with their signature moves,
making her fall in love all over again).

(9/15/19)

56

I want to tell you I'm sorry
for how I used to be and
how long it took for

me to change —

you were right to leave when you did;
even though I'm a better man
now there was just no forgiving how things where
when I acted like I didn't know any different

and the emotional pain grew on you
like the love you used to have for me.

Maybe it would have been different had
things not happened so
close together — but that's all just
speculation, and I cannot
do by what

could've been, even when it hurts to say it out loud.

You were the best thing to ever
happen to e; I can say that
now, and the truth will set me free,

but none of that changes the fact
that what's done is done, and so are you.

(We can't change the past
but we can always do better.)

(9/18/19)

57

I walk a couple of miles a day
because my doctor told me to drop
some weight if I wanted to
keep living and not die.

He meant only to shake me up and
alert me to the dangers of going down
the way I've been going; he
means well so I forgive him for

using death as a way of striking
at the root of the problem —
besides, I lost ten pounds so far
so it's not like it didn't work.

(9/18/19)

58

Mother I love you
even when I fuss and fight
like I did when I was a child —

you pulled me out of the fire
before I could get burned,
and you fed me with

love before sending me back
out into the world and letting me
stand upright again, like the man

I am soon becoming.

(9/18/19)

59

We are supposed to be stewards of
the earth—but look at how we
care for each other, and tell me if you think
our stewarding skills are sorely lacking.

(9/18/19)

60

Open the door leading out
into the dark, and then step out into your
winter Eden and head north of here—

I swear you will come to a kind of
religious experience sooner or
later; one where all your dreams come true and
nothing really ever happens to the good
who wait to hear the voice of

God fall down like specks of snow.

(9/18/19)

61

Bukowski liked to talk about
the bluebird in his heart;
he was afraid of people finding out
about it, and the effect it would have
on his life and art.

I don't know why he was
so scared, and to be honest
his edge could've used

some dulling on the blade
in the last years of his life when
everything else looked
bleak and the words weren't

cutting like they used to
in the barrooms where he

slowly drank himself to death.

If I were I him I would've

learned how to train the bird to
work for me —

the work I did thereafter
would probably be
a little bit better, and to see that thing
fly away would be worth the price
of owning and maintaining it

for the rest of it's
natural life.

Bukowski liked to talk about
his bird like it was a
cancer needing to be taken out
of him and thrown away;

was he insane?

Most men would kill
just to have the gut to admit
that they have that kind of

animal lurking around

inside of them.

Bukowski doesn't have a
clue what he's talking
about, and maybe that's why
he had to die early, so that
the animal didn't look

inside him and see
the pain that birthed him,

showing him that pain was
the only true love there
ever was.

Whatever it was, I guess we'll never know.

(9/18/19)

62

I don't like to talk about
my feelings
even though she said that it
was my feelings that first
got her to wanting to

talk to me back when we met

on the front steps of the
church where my old man does
the preaching and
where I got baptized.

She seems to know better than I, so
I don't try and fight it so much

anymore—she's got me
pegged to the last word, and
she knows she could have me

in any shape or form,

which makes me feel kind of
funny but I don't fight it
like I would've done a few years
ago when I wasn't so sure in

who I was or what I did
just to survive the next hour.

All of which is to say she's
got me where she wants me but
I'm not complaining.

(9/18/19)

63

It was an occasion of sin
that first got you into this mess,
but you have a circle of friends
who were like
older brothers to you
and two parents who'll understand
if you come back after losing
your way —

you're not too far gone
to come on back
into that place that's not unlike
your mother's embrace, and
not unlike the bed where

you first learned to
brave the monsters.

(9/18/19)

64

Goodbye friend,
thank you for listening to
me while I was far along
in my own head and
couldn't really
make it back to
where I needed to
be (which

definitely was not where
I was at the time).

Goodbye friend,
and please tell your wife and
kids I love them with
everything that's left of me
to give, with every
fiber of my being and
so long as I still
live and can

remember what the feeling
does to those who can
still feel.

Goodbye friend,
and please don't forget
me after I leave and
venture off into other places
and in other people's
company; they don't mean
as much to me as you do
and you know that
full well by
now.

Goodbye friend,
thank you for being where
I could know how to
find you as I needed you
(how lucky I am to
be able to see
you now) —

I may not be able

to pay you back as soon
as I would like,
but I know well enough to
hold on to the receipt
for when I can
reverse my
fortune

and pay it forward
on the next friend who
goes down on his luck.

(9/18/19)

ABOUT THE AUTHOR

James Lawson Moore is a poet and writer from Chesterfield, Virginia. Having studied English and Literature at Regent University, he now divides his time between his home town and Norfolk and Virginia Beach. His previous books include *The Journal of a Wannabe Artist* and *On the Run with Mike and Gunn*; he is also a screenwriter, with multiple scripts under his belt and circulating the indie circuit.

You can reach him at his personal Facebook page, entitled "James Moore, the Wannabe Artist." He's also on Twitter, under the "creative" Twitter handle @soggybottompoet.

Closing remarks from a man who talks too much...

This book comprises of the journey our boy took to reach a level of calm that can only be found within the pages of creative expression, the zen-like center a soul enters when the word is all that matters to him. He writes with a mix of honesty and tenderness, never allowing for one to overtake the other at any given time.

 Subjects include love, faith, death, and guilt, engaging in the creative act and even exploring through series of random philosophical tangents that one explores when the nights get long and sleep doesn't seem like a viable option at the time. Even when it appears as though he's not taking it seriously, the author has a reverence for the art, and everything written in this book is done with faith and humility.

 The artist evolves right before your eyes between the covers of this book. The artist's soul changes, morphs and shifts like the waves of weather-torn sands along the banks of the lower shore. He crafts an entire work, comprised of individual numbered pieces, that is entirely devoted to the sum total of human experience. Believing in God and man in equal measure, the artist strives to cultivate some kind of religious epiphany.

 Above all, the art perseveres.

www.ingramcontent.com/pod-product-compliance
Lightning Source LLC
Chambersburg PA
CBHW022113090426
42743CB00008B/831